TOLEDO

EVEREST

Text: José Luis Rodríguez Zapata

Photographs: Miguel Sánchez and Puri Lozano
Miguel Raurich
Archivo Everest

Editorial coordination: Francisco Bargiela

Diagrams: Gerardo Rodera

Cover Design: Alfredo Anievas

Cartography: © Everest

Translation: Alfredo Álvarez

© EDITORIAL EVEREST, S.A.
Carretera León-La Coruña, km 5 – LEÓN
ISBN: 84-241-3458-3
Legal deposit: LE. 351-1998
Printed in Spain

EDITORIAL EVERGRÁFICAS, S.L.
Carretera León-La Coruña, km 5
LEÓN (Spain)

TOLEDO

THE COAT OF ARMS

The city's current coat of arms has been built up from the age-old emblematic tradition of a seated emperor and a two-headed eagle. Its heraldic description is the following: a great two-headed eagle in the centre and to right and left an emperor seated on his throne with a cape of gold and an imperial crown likewise of gold; in his right hand each holds a silver sword and in his left a gold sceptre.

Castle of San Servando.

Side page:
the Puente
de Alcántara.

The seated figures of the kings or emperors are turned slightly towards the eagle. Over the heads of the eagle sits a gold imperial crown. The sable eagle, wings spread, has beak and talons of Gules, the latter armed in gold. In the centre stands the Spanish shield, quarterly one and four in Gules, a golden castle masoned in sable and surrounded by azure, 2 and 3 of silver with a rampant lion in Gules crowned in gold, langued and armed likewise. Silver-based nebuly with a pomegranate of the same colour colour, lined in Gules, worked and leafed with two vert leaves. The shield is ringed by the necklace of the Order of the Golden Fleece comprising twin links, interlaced with azure stones and flames in Gules, in the end hanging therefrom, a ramskin wreathed down the middle in gold.

THE HISTORICAL BACKGROUND

Toledo's particular setting on a hill girded by the sluggish River Tagus, together with its strategic position at the crossroads of many important communication routes, have made it a city charged with history from the distant times of Carpetania.
On this hill the Celtiberian civilisations built a series of forts, which then served as the basis for the establishment of a first walled *Celtiberian* town.
Conquered by the Romans in 192 BC, it was then reconstructed under the name of *Toletum* as part of the Carthaginian province.
After Barbarian incursions the walls were rebuilt for greater defence. By 306 it was already an episcopal see. In 411 it was taken by the Alani who were in turn defeated by the Goths in 418. Shortly after the start of the Visigoth rein in Spain, Atanagildo set up the court in Toledo in 554, and

Side page:
Puente de Alcántara.

under Leovigildo it then became the capital of the Hispanic Gothic Kingdom and an Archbishopric. In the Third Council of Toledo in 589 King Recaredo became a convert to Catholicism, thereby sparking off intense Monastic activity and a cultural renaissance with the building of many churches.

Conquered by the Arabs in 711, it lost its status as capital and became a dependency of Cordoba until 1012, when, after the breaking up of the Cordoba Caliphate, it became part of the Reinos de Taifas (petty kingdoms). It was then reconquered by the Christian King Alfonso VI in 1085. The city's great racial and linguistic diversity, with Mozarabs (Arabised Christians), Jews and Muslims all living harmoniously together, led to the setting up of a Translator's School in the C13th, under the keen stewardship of Alfonso X, *the wise*. Although the Muslim and Jewish populations were suffered to practice their own religious rituals, the Christians finally transformed the mosque into a cathedral. In the C15th Toledo became an important Castilian textile centre.

Following double page: general view of Toledo.

Hospital of Tavera.

The Jewish community made a significant contribution to the city's economic development, only to be expelled in 1492. The Catholic Monarchs, Ferdinand and Isabela, extended and developed Toledo. It was one of the first cities to rise up in defence of its own rights against Carlos I in the "Guerra de las Comunidades". Carlos I then made it the centre of his empire and built the Alcázar or Fortress. The C16th was one of the most prosperous for the city due to the boom of the Castilian textile industry, but the transfer of the Capital to Madrid in 1563 caused the city to fall into a decline that was then exacerbated further during the last Hapsburg rulers, although the founding of the Royal Company of Trade and Factories in 1748 caused a brief upturn in the city's fortunes up to 1827. Since 1983 Toledo has been the capital of the Junta de Comunidades de Castilla-La Mancha, the regional community.

THE CITY OF THE THREE CULTURES

The age-old city of Toledo, and the sights to be seen there, are clearly marked by the confluence of three different cultures: Toledo's is the unique personality corresponding to a town in which three monotheistic cultures have lived side by side: Christian, Arab and Hebrew.
Almost all Toledo's important buildings are religious in character; around every corner the visitor will stumble upon churches, monasteries, hermitages or religious schools corresponding in their origins to one of the three aforementioned cultures. Since these buildings are scattered throughout the whole maze of its narrow, higgledy-piggledy streets, there are various ways of wandering around and chancing upon this evidence of its glorious past. We are going to lay down here a basic itinerary to take in the outstanding spots and give as complete an overview as possible, brief though it may be, of the city.

Before entering the city's historical centre, clearly marked out by a looping gorge of the river Tagus and the walls of the city, it would be just as well to take a stroll around the ring road that runs along the opposite bank of the Tagus for a first, panoramic view of its origin and subsequent development.
The basic route through Toledo starts next to its main gate, the *Puerta de Bisagra*, where the **Church of Santiago del Arrabal** stands, perhaps the most important example of Mudejar architecture in Toledo (Christian architecture under Moorish influence). Its oldest part is the C12th tower, and the most important of its three doorways, all adorned with interlaced or lobed arches, is that located at the lower end of the church with a horseshoe arch framed in an Arabic alfiz. Its interior, both in the nave and the aisles, is covered with a Mudejar roof; the most interesting objects are a C16th Plateresque altarpiece, several tombstones and a C14th Mudejar pulpit.

The wall.

Three views of
the Church of
Santiago del Arrabal.

From the church of Santiago we follow Calle Real Del Arrabal towards the city centre, taking some stairs on the right that lead to the *Puerta de Valmardón.* Passing beneath the gate's arch we find on the left the **Mosque of Cristo de la Luz,** one of the architectural gems of Muslim Toledo. Over the remains of a Visigoth church the Arabs raised in 1000 a mosque called Valmardón, which then became converted into a Mudejar church in the C12th under the name of Cristo de la Luz: the legend behind its name (Christ of the Light) dates back to the reconquest of Toledo by Alfonso VI. When the city had been taken the king entered it through the Puerta de Bisagra, and when he was passing in front of the mosque, the point marked by a

white stone, his horse collapsed to the ground and refused to rise again. Considering this to have some sort of supernatural cause, the king ordered the spot to be dug up, and inside the mosque a crucifix was found with a small, lighted oil lamp, which had apparently been burning throughout the Muslim domination of the city.

The main front of Cristo de la Luz comprises three different arches framed in crossed blind arches and a line of rhombi supporting a frieze with cufic characters. Inside, the columns, mostly Visigoth in origin, support a superimposed arcade as in the Mosque of Cordoba. Its nine different domes are in the Arabic Caliphal style, and inside the Mozarabic church there are vestiges of Romanesque paintings.

We retrace our steps beneath the arch of Valmardón and go back down the steps to continue to the right down the same street as before. Before getting to the Cuesta de las Armas we will find the magnificent

Puerta del Sol, a C14th Mudejar work that functioned as the Medina entrance and formed part of the city's second wall.

We go further down the same street and find on the left the Paseo del Miradero, with handsome views over the banks of the Tagus. The Paseo del Miradero is overlooked by the windows of the **Convento de Santa Fe,** which occupies part of the old Palacios de Galiana, built by the Muslim governors and rulers within the fortified part of the city. The convent was built by order of King Alfonso VI. Its apse has survived to this day, as has the well-known C11th *Capilla de Belén,* which is a small square whose interior is converted into an octagon covered by a Caliphal vault, the ribs of which do not meet in the centre, supported on eight stout horseshoe arches. Inside the chapel is buried Fernán Pérez, son of Fernando III, *el Santo,* whose tomb is adorned with Mozarab plasterwork. There are also C15th paintings and a fine ceiling of the same era with a beautiful Moorish alfarje (wood panelling). At the end of the Cuesta de las Armas we come to the **Plaza de Zocodover,** in the olden days a market place and today the nerve centre of Toledo and meeting point of its inhabitants. Three sides of this square are arcaded, and it is the hub of several lively streets that lead off to other parts of the city.

The east facade has the *Arco de la Sangre,* an Arab gate from the first military enclosure, through which we get to the **Hospital and Museum of Santa Cruz,** founded by Cardinal Pedro González de Mendoza, who wished to bring together in a single building the various hospitals of Toledo. It was built from 1504 to 1514 in the Plateresque style, as may be witnessed both in its doorway and in the detailed decoration covering the windows, while the interior courtyard, in whose construction Alonso de Covarrubias took part, corresponds to a more advanced Renaissance style. Its

Puerta del Sol. ▶

Alcázar of Toledo.
General view.

14

interior boasts a magnificent stairway leading up to the second floor, totally covered by Plateresque decoration that overflows onto banisters, pilasters and bolsters of the facing wall, plus some fine coffered ceilings. This building currently houses a *Provincial Museum* divided into three sections: archaeology, fine arts and decorative arts.

Doorway of the Hospital de la Santa Cruz.

**Above, stairway of the Hospital-Museum of Santa Cruz.
Different aspects of the Alcázar de Toledo.**

The Cuesta de Carlos V takes us to the glacis of the Alcázar, a historical site that served in the past as a Roman courtyard, Muslim citadel and royal palace. The first Christian fortress of the **Alcázar** was constructed at the behest of Alfonso VI after reconquering the city and its first governor was El Cid. In the C13th it was reformed and acquired the layout we see today, although King Carlos III later decided to build his residence here, and in the C18th and C19th it was restored after the damage caused by the wars of succession and independence, thereafter being reduced to a ruin during the siege of the Spanish Civil War. Its main front is by Covarrubias and the southern facade by Juan de Herrera; the four facades together form a regular floor plan with a central courtyard flanked by four square projecting towers. In its interior there is a magnificent courtyard with two galleries of columns and semi-circular arches decorated with imperial shields and a handsome staircase covered with barrel vaults. Its rooms house offices and an *Army Museum*.

We now turn our steps back to the Plaza de Zocodover and make directly for the cathedral down Calle de Comercio, which abounds in many shops with typical Toledo products and mementoes, and then we continue down the prolongation of the latter, Calle del Hombre de Palo. The **Cathedral** is Toledo's most characteristic building, and its architecture reflects almost the entire Spanish Gothic art, since it took over two hundred years to build, from 1227 to 1493. This primate cathedral is in fact a rich collection of works of art and a museum of exceptional value. It stands on the site of an old Visigoth church dedicated to Santa María, over which Toledo's main mosque was then built during Muslim domination.

From the Plaza del Ayuntamiento we can take in the majesty of its construction with its main front framed with two towers of different heights, since only the left one was finished and built up to the full height of ninety metres. In its interior is the well known Campana Gorda or Great Bell, which weighs in at 17,744 kilograms. It was cast in the C18th and its first peals shattered many windows throughout the city and the bell itself fractured almost immediately.

The three doorways in this main front are the Puerta del Perdón in the centre and the Puerta del Infierno and the Puerta del Juicio at the sides, their names (Forgiveness, Hell and Judgement) reflected in their tympanum scenes. The usual entrance for visiting the cathedral is the Puerta del Mollete beside the main tower under the covered way linking the archbishop's palace and the cathedral. This door leads into

Sala de las batallas
(battle room)
in the Alcázar.

Side page:
view of
the Cathedral.

Toledo Cathedral.
Side page: the
Puerta del Perdón.
Right: the southern
arm of the crossing.

the C14th cloister and then through the Puerta de la Presentación into the cathedral itself, formed by a central nave and four aisles divided by pillars from which the ribs soar up to support the Gothic ribbed vaults. The nave is higher than the aisles and has great windows with stained glass; the aisles carry on round the main altar to form a double ambulatory with a tribune of multi-lobed arches and seven apses with chapels in between. Our tour of the cathedral can begin to the left of its entrance to visit the *Sacristía*, which harbours part of the *Cathedral Museum*, with a wealth of pictures, jewels and precious metal work. On the other side of the ambulatory is the *Sala Capitular* (Chapter House) with its Cisneros-style doorway giving onto a gate and then the room itself. Its magnificent coffered ceiling from 1508 was done in the Renaissance Mudejar style, while the walls are decorated with frescoes by

The Transparente in the ambulatory, and the main altarpiece.

Juan de Borgoña. In the centre of the ambulatory we suddenly find that the Gothic harmony of the building is ruptured by a grandiose Baroque construction: the famous *Transparente,* formed by a sumptuous altar piece of three marble sections. Sunlight pours down from a hole punched in the vault, thereby illuminating directly the tabernacle and highlighting the choir of angels and clouds surrounding the Blessed Sacrament. Behind the Transparente we come to the *Capilla Mayor* (Main Altar), which has a great flamboyant C16th altarpiece, plus the Renaissance-style tomb of Cardinal Mendoza. The royal tombs of Alfonso VII and Berenguela lie on one side of the presbytery and those of Sancho and María de Molina on the other. Directly opposite stands the *Coro* (Choir) whose lower part has magnificent wooden stalls carved in the late C15th with scenes reflecting the reconquest of Granada. This choir also has an C18th organ and a splendid C13th marble image of the Virgen Blanca. At the end of the south aisle, beneath a small tower, is the *Capilla Mozárabe* or *Capilla del Corpus Christi*, designated in 1504 by Cardinal Cisneros to be the chapel where the mass according to Mozarabic rites was to be preserved, and it is still celebrated according to this liturgy on every Sunday. Last but not least in our cathedral visit is the *Tesoro Catedralicio* (Cathedral Treasury) in the Capilla de San Juan, located next to the entrance under the great tower. This chapel has a fine Plateresque doorway and inside there is an exhibition of many pieces of religious precious metalwork. The highlight is the gigantic C16th *Custodia* or Monstrance made of solid silver, gold and precious stones, nearly four metres high and weighing over 200 kilos. Inside this custodia is another one that was owned by the Catholic monarchs and was gilded

Following double page: the choir.

with the first gold brought by
Columbus from the new world. This
custodia is paraded through the city
on the day of Corpus Christi, the
streets duly decked out with
awnings and tapestries and carpeted
with thyme, lavender and rosemary.
We leave the cathedral by the Puerta
del Mollete again to make our way to
the Plaza del Ayuntamiento, where
we will find the Casa Consistorial
(City Hall) and Palacio Arzobispal
(Archbishop's Palace) with a fine
doorway in florid Gothic style.
A stairway between the Archbishop's
Palace and the City Hall leads us to
the Plaza del Consistorio, from
where we go down the Pasadizo del
Ayuntamiento to the Callejón de
Santa Ursula. In this alleyway we can
observe the apse of the **Church of
Santa Úrsula** in Toledo Mudejar
style. At the end of the alleyway we
turn right into Calle de Santa Ursula.
Before getting to the Plaza del
Salvador on the left we take the

Calle del Taller del Moro, where, a
few metres on the right, stands the
museum of the **Taller del Moro**
(Moorish Workshop), built in the
C14th. Here we can see a great
rectangular room with a lot of
plasterwork decoration using
geometric and plant motifs and the
central room covered in alfarjes and
the side rooms decorated with
Mozarabic themes. In the Plaza del
Salvador we turn left into Calle de
Santo Tomé. On the left we find the
Church of **Santo Tomé,**
reconstructed in the early C14th. To
enter and see the famous painting of
The *Burial of Conde de Orgaz,* we go
down an alleyway in the very tower
of this church called Travesía del
Conde. This picture was painted by
El Greco in about 1586 and
represents a Toledo legend of the
C14th, according to which St.
Augustine and St. Stephen came
down from heaven to lower the
Count into the tomb. The picture can

Toledo cathedral.
Above, sala Capitular
(Chapter House).
Side page: capilla de
Santiago (above)
and Sacristía Mayor,
with works by El Greco,
pride of place going to
"El expolio" (below).

Left:
torre de Santo Tomé.

Right: casa del Greco.

Different views of the Synagogue
of El Transito.

Above, casa del Greco.
El Greco's
"Burial of the Conde de Orgaz".

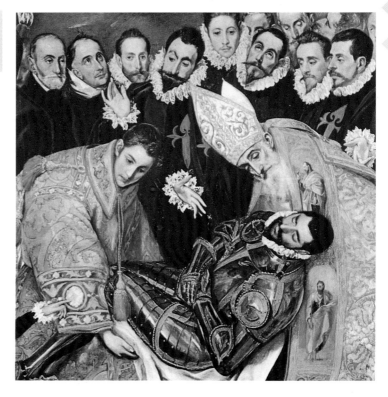

30

be broken down compositionally into two distinct zones. The lower part is the burial attended by a group of people who are portraits of the painter's contemporaries, whereas the upper part is the glory composed by Christ, the Virgin and Saint John the Baptist who prepare to receive him. Next to this church stands the C15th Palacio de Fuensalida. In front of the Church of Santo Tomé we now take the Calle de San Juan de Dios to go down to our next port of call, the Casa del Greco.

A small alley called "Calle de Samuel Levi" on the left leads directly to it. The present **Casa del Greco,** the house in which the inspired artist lived on two occasions, is a C14th Moorish house. Today it is a museum housing several of his paintings. After this visit we carry on down Calle Samuel Levi to the **Synagogue of El Transito,** which is part of the palace constructed in 1366 by the Jew who has given his name to the street, Samuel Levi, the treasurer of Pedro I of Castile. The building's exterior is Mudejar in style and the interior stands out for the richness of its decoration. The wall of the upper end is totally covered with plasterwork; the triple arcade in the centre is for the Ark containing the Torah scroll. Along the whole upper part runs a plasterwork frieze, and above this is an ornamental top of lobed arches over coloured marble

columns. The ceiling has a magnificent octagonal loopwork alfarje. Today, in adjacent rooms, a *Sephardic Museum* has been set up, with various exhibits of the Jewish culture in Spain.

Leaving the Synagogue del Transito, we take the Calle de los Reyes Católicos on the right to reach the Synagogue of **Santa María la Blanca.** This synagogue, set almost in the dead centre of the Jewish quarter, is a late C12th building, refurbished after a fire in the C13th.

It is the great Jewish synagogue par excellence. The interior comprises a nave and four aisles divided by totally whitewashed horseshoe arches, and the ceiling conserves the original alfarje wood panelling. These arches rest on remarkable column capitals, all different and adorned with great pineapples. In the mid C16th the synagogue was transformed into a Christian church and three chapels were added at the upper end. It conserves a Plateresque main altar.

San Juan de los Reyes: general view.

Detail of the apse of San Juan de los Reyes.

We now continue down Calle de los Reyes Católicos to the Church of **San Juan de los Reyes.** This work was commissioned from Juan Guas by the Catholic Monarchs, Ferdinand and Isabella, to commemorate their victory in the Battle of Toro over the supporters of the Infanta Juana la Beltraneja. It is one of the best examples of Hispanic-Flemish or Isabelline Gothic art. The most notable features of the exterior are an openwork balustrade, several pinnacles and an octagonal tambour. The chains hanging from one of the walls are those of the

Christians liberated from the Muslims. The church interior consists of a single nave and stands out for its sculptural decoration. A sort of frieze runs the length of the nave separating the upper and lower part of the church; at the crossing it forms two tribunes originally built for the Catholic Monarchs. A door gives on to a magnificent two-storey cloister: the lower floor is ogival and the upper Plateresque, crowned by a balustrade and pinnacles. The upper galleries are covered with a fine Mudejar coffered ceiling from the C15th.

THE CORPUS CHRISTI PROCESSION

The Corpus Christi procession in Toledo is an "Auto Sacramental" (traditional religious play) that takes to the streets. The city is decked out with awnings and tapestries and carpeted with aromatic herbs while, in an act full of colour and replete with spirituality, the magnificent early C16th Custodia Procesional (Processional Monstrance) of Enrique de Arfe is ceremoniously paraded through the streets. Eighteen kilos of gold, one hundred and eighty three kilos of gilded silver and a host of precious stones making up a grand total of five thousand six hundred pieces and twelve thousand five hundred screws were used to make this gem. On this auspicious day it is ceremoniously paraded through the narrow streets arrayed with thyme and lavender, with awnings sprinkled by spring showers to the sound of stifled sighs on balconies covered with Philippine silk shawls,

Four views of
San Juan de los Reyes.

Detail of the Custodia
(Monstrance) of
Enrique de Arfe. ▶

Ayuntamiento (City Hall) of Toledo decked out for the Corpus Christi procession and the mayor and council officials taking part in the procession.

Damascene work.

**Corpus Christi in Toledo:
the Plaza de Zocodover
duly adorned
and a view of
the procession itself.**

past solders standing stock still from dawn onwards, with deafening rockets, giants recalling the four continents, pealing bells, Dutch tapestries, aromatic incense. This whole world of emotions is revived by Toledo people each year so that God, though the medium of their Custodia de Arfe, wrought from the first gold brought from South America, may feel the vibrant, throbbing expression of people who remain steadfast in their faith.

The origins of this magnificent procession date back to the C12th and C13th, when the Alibi heretics were refuting the doctrine of transubstantiation and more and more people were abandoning the Holy Communion. Pope Gregory III therefore convoked the Council of Letran in 1215 to lay down the way that the "Easter Communion" should be performed, with the bread to be taken kneeling and in the mouth, not in the hand as before the C11th.

From this moment on the Popes laid great stress on the Eucharist until turning this date into the *fiesta* par excellence of Christianity on the day "when the sun shines brightest". Imperial Toledo, in imitation of Papal Rome, took to the narrow streets and squares with their Primate at the head to parade the Host through the city, just as Pope Nicholas V did for the first time in 1447 in the "Eternal City" of Rome. Under the patronage of the monarchs or the cardinals, the protection of the nobles, with the collaboration of the guilds and, above all, the spirituality and verve of the people, Toledo has gradually enhanced the splendour of this liturgical procession, which leaves both locals and visitors open-mouthed in admiration.

DAMASCENE WORK

The pinnacle of Toledo craftsmanship is its damascene work. Persian in origin, it was introduced in the Caliphal Court in the C10th but Toledo swordsmiths were soon turning out work of such quality that the very art

Toledo offers
the visitor a wide
range of typical
articles.

became synonomous with these Tagus-tempered weapons. Initially it was the work of Mudejars. The technique involves cutting a grooved pattern into the metal, where the craftsman will then inlay the gold or silver thread so that, once blended in, it will bring out the contrast between this thread of precious metal and the blued, less noble base metal, such as iron, bronze steel or copper. Damascene work is carried out on items as diverse as plates, bracelets, rings, tiepins, broaches, etc.

GASTRONOMY

Toledo is the urban centre of a region rich in the finest vegetable products, and it has long been such an important communication crossroads that the most varied selection of spices, fish and salted food have been naturalised as true Toledo products for centuries. It also does a fine line in oils and wines. But above all Toledo is open country, and it boasts the title of the world's top region in both small game species, such as partridge, hare and quail, and the big game species such

Preceding double page: "View of Toledo" by El Greco.

as deer and wild boar. Toledo's forte is its stewed partridge, slowly cooked and served up with steamed potatoes laced with black chocolate to liven up the sauce and make it smoother. Other typical dishes are "cuchifrito" (lamb, tomato, egg, saffron and white wine), partridge with beans, "carcamusa" and "tortilla a la magra" (ham omelette). But without doubt the quintessential Toledo food product is its *marzipan*. Marzipan goes back a long way in Toledo. Legend has it that during the siege of Toledo by Alfonso VI the city ran completely out of food and the people were afflicted by a terrible hunger. Some Toledo Muslims discovered sacks of almonds and sugar in a basement. They milled both products, mixed them with a little water, shaped them into balls and baked them, thereby inventing marzipan. Although it is made all the year round it becomes a veritable city industry at Christmas.

As for wine there are two different types: the "manchego" or La Mancha wines and the "rougher" reds of Méntrida.

TOLEDO AND EL GRECO

El Greco must be understood as a Greek artist who became not so much Spanish but "Toledan" in particular, because it was Toledo's oriental stamp, its unique form of Byzantine Orientalism, that most attracted him to the city. The painter Dominico Theotocópuli "El Greco" came to Toledo in 1577, and his encounter with its tortured horizons, with its magic and mystery, represented an epoch-changing event for Spanish art. EL Greco was an educated man, ironic and sybarite in his habits, who painted Toledo in two ways: one precise, almost realistic, the other more idealised. The best works of the Cretan artist remain in the city and its province, which thereby becomes the museum of his painting. Toledo shows the masterworks of El Greco with pride, and very close to the painter's dwelling stands the House and Museum of El Greco, with an important collection of his works, the highlight of which is "View of Toledo".

LIVING IN TOLEDO

Until we have entered the houses of Toledo we can't really be said to know it. The most typical Toledo houses stand on the foundations of the old Arab, Hebrew, Visigoth and even Roman houses. These are two or three storey buildings with a central courtyard with spaces for stables, caves or basements. Many are adorned with plasterwork, and the upper floors were originally open galleries that were closed off to turn them into rooms. Mention must also be made of the "cigarrales" country houses surrounding the city across the river, traditionally used by Toledo people as summer or weekend residences. Today they are occupied not only by locals but by all those who love the imperial city.

The "cigarral" or rural house.

Toledo by night. ▶

On these pages:
various views of
old Toledo.

46

THE SPIRIT OF TOLEDO

Quiet, secluded squares, sturdy mansions, a tangle of steep, narrow streets forming a veritable maze. In the doorways, many coats of arms and crests: quiet, age-old suburbs. A multitude of buildings and, as the hub of everyday life, the open Plaza de Zocodover.

A good deal of Toledo's attraction resides in its miraculous urban layout, in which the ruins of the old Jewish area add their dash of magic. It smacks at once of fortitude, hauteur, melancholy, plenitude and mysticism. Redolent of broom and incense, just as it was painted by El Greco.

Cervantes put his finger on the spirit of this symbolic city. That "winsome outcrop, glory of Spain and light of its cities" is the most exact, eternal definition.

Toledo hoards echoes from Spain's glorious past, ranging from the artful wiles of "La Celestina", through the magic feats of the Marquis of Vallena, the grandeur of King Alfonso X the Wise to the doctrinal arguments of Juan Manuel.

Its silent corners still seem to ring with the echoes of all the public figures that have laid the foundations of its amorous, heroic, knightly legend. Past and present in a timeless eternity.

COMMERCIAL TRADITION

In 1592 the royal mayor Juan Gutierrez Tello was responsible for an important piece of Toledo town planning: he ordered the commercial area to be built, reformed Zocodover and widened the Plaza Mayor.

Today the commercial area stretching from Zocodover to the cathedral is still the heart of Toledo's economic activity.

Shops of all kinds, cafés and banks are heavily concentrated in this lively spot. Four centuries ago Zocodover (an Arabic word meaning "place of the animals") was home to artisans and a Tuesday market was held for centuries until being moved only a few years ago to the Paseo Del Carmen.

It also staged bullfights, there were games of "cucañas" or climbing a greasy pole, autos da fe were held here and malefactors put to death. The Calle de Comercio led off from Zocodover, as it still does today. It contained chairmaker's workshops, brassworkers, ironworkers, jewellers,

ropemakers, halter-makers and the shops of the king. This Calle de Comercio finished, and still finishes, in Cuatro Calles, where the old "Alcaicería" (silk warehouse) stood. Like so many other things in Toledo, it is virtually unchanged.